Finding a RAINBOW through the Rain

A GRIEF JOURNAL & WORKBOOK FOR THE LOSS OF A HUSBAND

Carolyn's Dream Publishing

In Memory Of Al

" I have fought the good fight,
I have finished the race.
I have kept the faith."
2 Timothy 4:7

to my husband in heaven,

I was supposed to spend the rest of my life with you. And then I realized you spent the rest of your life with me. I smile because I know you loved me till the day you went away. And will keep loving me....

till the day we're together again
From: Your Love!

Introduction

July 8th, A day that changed my life forever...

My husband and partner of 46 years passed away unexpectedly. To this day I am still trying to process it. We all go through different degrees of grief, for some it may be never coming out of your room. For others it may be putting on a smile and acting as if nothing happened at all.

For me I felt myself slipping into a dark place where I didn't want to be. I had family and friends around me and supporting me but it wasn't enough. This was something I had to work on myself. One night as I laid in bed asking God why can't I move past this? I heard a voice say because your not remembering the good times. I kept that in my head for weeks.

One night as I was watching TV a commercial came on from a famous food chain. "Hey Good Lookin" was playing and I could picture my husband doing this silly dance. A few moments later I remembered the warmth of his hand on my shoulder every time he would pass me as I sat in my computer chair. More and more I started remembering the good times we had together instead of focusing on the negative past.

"When someone you love
becomes a memory,
the memory becomes
a treasure"
-Unknown

Introduction

I started talking more with my family about the good times and we would find ourselves laughing till all hours of the morning about some of our silly antics. Then I started writing down all the memories I would have, from the first day we met to his last day here.

And that is where you come in. See there are so many memories we sometimes forget during our grief. That's why I created this journal and workbook with prompted questions for you to answer. Bring some of that joy back into your life. Remember all the good times every time you open your book. May it comfort you as well as it comforted me writing it.

Carol

"Once in a while right in the middle of an ordinary life, love gives us a Fairytale"
-Unknown

There is no right or wrong way to go about this book.

Follow your heart.

Answer each question or only the ones that spark a memory for you.

Take a day, take a month, take a year. It's up to you.

My hope is that you find peace and joy through the process of reliving your favorite memories with your husband and....

This Page Intentionally Left Blank

Where did you meet?

Add photos, memorabilia, ticket stubs, etc

Where was your first date?

"I'll always love you like it's the beginning"
-Unknown

Where was your favorite place to go?

"Where there is love
there is life"
-Mahatma Gandhi

What was their favorite food and is there a story to go with it?

Notes

What was one of your funniest moments together?

"When it rains look
for rainbows
when it's dark
look for stars"
-Oscar Wilde

What was a hobby you both enjoyed?

Add photos, memorabilia, ticket stubs, etc

Was there a famous person they wanted to meet and why?

"Hold on to the love
not the loss"
-Eva Longoria

What was his favorite T.V. show?

"For the rest of my life
I will search for moments
full of you"
-Unknown

What was one of your family traditions?

Add photos, memorabilia, ticket stubs, etc

What is something that made you angry but you can laugh about it now?

"Life! What art thou
without love"
-E. Moore

What were one of your happiest moments together?

"Love makes all
the negative thoughts
disappear"
-Unknown

What attracted you to your husband?

Notes

Describe his laugh?

"Don't cry because it's over,
smile because it happened"
-Dr. Seuss

What meaningful advice did your husband give?

"At the touch of love
everyone becomes
a poet"
-Plato

Who said I love you first?

"No matter where you are
he'll always be watching
over you. He will stay with
you forever"
-Unknown

When and where did you have your first kiss?

"Many waters cannot
quench love,
neither can the floods
drown it"
-Old Testament
Solomon's Song

What scent reminds you of your husband?

If it is a cologne or
aftershave put a dab
on the paper. The scent
will last for years to come

Notes

<u>*Finding a Rainbow through the Rain*</u>

Describe your Wedding Day

"And so together
they built a life
they loved"
-Unknown

Did you have a wedding song?
If you did what was it?

"It was not my lips
you kissed but
my soul"
-Judy Garland

How did you know you were in love?

Add photos, memorabilia, ticket stubs, etc

How did your husband propose and did you go on a honeymoon?

"I will keep your
love long in my heart
even after your gone"
-Unknown

If you have children what was your husband's reaction when he knew he was going to be a father?

"Perhaps they are not the
stars in the sky, but
rather openings where
our loved ones shine
down to let us know
they are happy"
-Eskimo Proverb

Describe a special Valentine's Day

"Christmas comes once a year
our love only comes once
in a lifetime"
-Unknown

What was one of your favorite Christmas presents your husband gave you?

"If snowflakes were
kisses from heaven
I would ask for a
blizzard"
-Unknown

Did you ever build a snowman or make snow angels together?

Notes

Describe your first home or apartment

"For the rest of
my life I will
search for
moments full
of you"
-Unknown

Was your husband good at fixing things around the house?

Add photos, memorabilia, ticket stubs, etc

Was your husband a good listener?

"There are some who bring a light so great to the world that even after they have gone the light remains"

-Unknown

Did your husband save for a rainy day or was he impulsive?

"Although it's difficult
today to see beyond
the sorrow, May
looking back in
memory help comfort
you tomorrow"
-Unknown

Did you and your husband go on leisurely drives?

"In the garden of memory, in the palace of dreams...that is where you and I shall meet"
-Alice Through the Looking Glass

What was one of the most fascinating places you and your husband visited ?

Notes

What did you and your husband do for fun? Dancing? Bowling? Go to the beach ?

"Memories. Let them
fill your mind,
warm your heart
and lead you
through"
-Unknown

Was your husband a good dancer ?

"Courage is not having
the strength to go on;
it is going on when you
don't have the strength"
-Theodore Roosevelt

What is one of your funniest stories together?

Add photos, memorabilia, ticket stubs, etc

Did your husband have a signature saying or quote?

"We shall find peace.
We shall hear angels,
we shall see the sky
sparkling with
diamonds"
-Anton Chekov

Did your husband enjoy reading?
Who were his favorite authors?

"It takes a minute to find
a special person, an hour to
appreciate them, and a day
to love them, but it takes
an entire lifetime to
forget them"
-Kahlil Gibran

Did your husband talk about any of his childhood friends?

"It's so much darker when
a light goes out, than it
would have been if it
had never shone"
-John Steinbeck

Is there a particular lesson you have learned from your husband?

"Being deeply loved by
someone gives you
strength, while loving
someone deeply gives
you courage"
-Lao Tzu

Did you have pet names for one another?

Notes

If your husband liked sports what were his favorite sports teams? Football? Baseball? Basketball?

"One word frees us of
all the weight and
pain of life:
that word is love"
-Sophocles

What kind of car did your husband drive? Can you associate good memories with a particular vehicle?

"Memories...Let them fill your mind, warm your heart, and lead you through"
-Unknown

Did your husband like animals?
If yes what was his favorite?

Add photos, memorabilia, ticket stubs, etc

What was your husbands idea of a romantic evening?

"When I tell you I love you, I am not saying it out of habit, I am reminding you that you are my life"
-Unknown

Was your husband mischievous?
Describe a memory if he was.

"And suddenly all the
love songs were about you"
-Unknown

Did your husband serve in the military? If so what branch of service was he in?

"Some people search their
whole lives to find what
I found in you"
-Unknown

What one word could describe their personality?

"Your my favorite place
to visit when my mind
searches for peace"
-Unknown

Was there a piece of clothing or jewelry they wore that was characteristic of them?

Notes

What was the best dream you achieved together?

"Whenever grief tries to
steal the beauty of
your memories, Just remember:
Love. Never. Dies"
-Unknown

Did your husband have any type of collections?

"I believe the hardest part
of healing after you've lost
someone you love it to
recover the "you" that went
away with them"
-Sharanya Brahmachari

Did he have a favorite possession?

"Grief is courage; to keep
stepping through a life
that feels like it ended"
-Unknown

Describe a perfect day with your husband

Add photos, memorabilia, ticket stubs, etc

What will you do to keep your husband's memory alive?

"The only people who
think there is a time
limit for grief, have
never lost a piece of
their heart
take all the time you need"
-Unknown

If you could ask any question
what would it be?
Write a letter to your husband when you
feel you are ready.

"When someone we love dies,
the hardest part is not
letting go of whom we
have lost, it's finding
the strength & courage
to move forward
without them"
-Unknown

Well that is it for the questions. I hope you have found some joy as I have reliving some of those precious moments in time, and the beauty of your relationship.

Use the following pages to journal any other thoughts you may have. Come back to this book over and over to relive the precious memories that you will always carry with you.

Finding a Rainbow through the Rain

Finding a Rainbow through the Rain

Finding a Rainbow through the Rain

Finding a Rainbow through the Rain

Finding a Rainbow through the Rain

Finding a Rainbow through the Rain

Finding a Rainbow through the Rain

Finding a Rainbow through the Rain

Finding a Rainbow through the Rain

Finding a Rainbow through the Rain

Finding a Rainbow through the Rain

Finding a Rainbow through the Rain

Finding a Rainbow through the Rain

Finding a Rainbow through the Rain

Finding a Rainbow through the Rain

Finding a Rainbow through the Rain

Finding a Rainbow through the Rain

Finding a Rainbow through the Rain

Finding a Rainbow through the Rain

Finding a Rainbow through the Rain

Finding a Rainbow through the Rain

Finding a Rainbow through the Rain

Finding a Rainbow through the Rain

Finding a Rainbow through the Rain

Finding a Rainbow through the Rain

Finding a Rainbow through the Rain

Finding a Rainbow through the Rain

Finding a Rainbow through the Rain

Finding a Rainbow through the Rain

Finding a Rainbow through the Rain

Finding a Rainbow through the Rain

Finding a Rainbow through the Rain

Finding a Rainbow through the Rain

Finding a Rainbow through the Rain

Finding a Rainbow through the Rain

Finding a Rainbow through the Rain

Finding a Rainbow through the Rain

Finding a Rainbow through the Rain

Finding a Rainbow through the Rain

Finding a Rainbow through the Rain

Finding a Rainbow through the Rain

Finding a Rainbow through the Rain

Finding a Rainbow through the Rain

Finding a Rainbow through the Rain

Finding a Rainbow through the Rain

Finding a Rainbow through the Rain

Finding a Rainbow through the Rain

Finding a Rainbow through the Rain

Finding a Rainbow through the Rain

Finding a Rainbow through the Rain